THE WRITER'S QUOTATION BOOK

THE WRITER'S QUOTATION BOOK

A · LITERARY · COMPANION

PUSHCART

EDITED BY JAMES CHARLTON

Library of Congress Card Number: 85-060721
ISBN: 0-916366-35-9

Manufactured in the United States of America
by RAY FREIMAN & COMPANY
Stamford, Connecticut 06903

Writers love quotations. They love quoting someone else's work almost as much as they love quoting their own. We consider a well-placed quotation, whether it be Shakespeare, Twain or Groucho Marx, to be one of the signs of an erudite and educated person. It lends weight to one's own opinions by somehow invoking a greater—or at least more well-known—authority.

Collecting quotations seems a similar occupation to the one practiced by those birds and animals who pick up shiny pebbles, pieces of glass and paper to line their nests and burrows. They discard one, pick up another, apparently at random, but all with a particular spot in mind. The result is a living place that conforms to their own sensibility and shape. Picking up bright and clever quotations, turning them over, scrutinizing them and finally placing them in a particular spot would undoubtedly get a chirp of approval.

This book started life as a modest 32-page giveaway at the 1980 American Booksellers Association convention, the annual bazaar where publishers hawk their wares. The publishing company, for which I was editor-in-chief at the time, needed some sort of handout to compete with the tote bags, t-shirts, posters and occasional book handed out during the four-day meeting.

Since I had accumulated a drawer full of quotations on publishing, the booklet was an easy idea to implement. To add to those, I asked a number of writers, editors, agents and friends to send me their favorites. What I thought was a solitary indulgence turned out to be a pastime practiced by a number of people involved with books. Aphorisms, witticisms, palindromes, bon mots, and gossip from the past and present poured in when I asked people to share their favorite literary sampler with me. The resulting booklet struck a responsive chord with booksellers and reviewers, and Bill Henderson of Pushcart Press asked me to expand it for a real publication. I was delighted to oblige.

Five years have passed since the first edition of The Writer's Quotation Book was published. It has been reviewed, quoted and plagiarized, adopted for school use, reprinted four times in hard cover, reprinted as a paperback, and selected by a book club. In the time the book has been available, a number of people have given me favorite quotations, sent me clippings, and suggested that the book be expanded. Bill Henderson, in his inimitable style, shrugged a 'why not?' when I suggested the idea of a revision and expansion.

Last month I discovered the idea behind The Writer's Quotation Book was not an original one. A friend sent a copy of a collection of quotations about books entitled Ex Libris published in 1936. The 54-page hard cover book was "printed, bound (and sold) at the First National Fair sponsored by the New York Times and the National Association of Book Publishers. Compiled at their request by Christopher Morley." But Mr. Morley's sensibility seems to be much more respectful and serious than mine, and every generation must reflect its own times and taste.

"To be amused by what you read—that is the great spring of happy quotations," penned C.E. Montague in A Writer's Notes To His Trade, and I think all writers, readers and their friends will find this book amusing, entertaining and instructive.

JAMES CHARLTON
New York City

THE WRITER'S QUOTATION BOOK

Literature was not born the day when a boy crying "wolf, wolf" came running out of the Neanderthal valley with a big gray wolf at his heels: literature was born on the day when a boy came crying "wolf, wolf" and there was no wolf behind him.

VLADIMIR NABOKOV

The last thing that we find in making a book is to know what we must put first.

BLAISE PASCAL

There is nothing so important as the book can be.

MAXWELL PERKINS

All that Mankind has done, thought, gained or been: it is lying as in magic preservation in the pages of books. They are the chosen possession of man.

THOMAS CARLYLE

It is a great thing to start life with a small number of really good books which are your very own.

SHERLOCK HOLMES

The walls of books around him, dense with the past, formed a kind of insulation against the present world and its disasters.

ROSS MAC DONALD

A room without books is like a body without soul.

CICERO

As good almost kill a man as kill a good book: who kills a man kills a reasonable creature, God's image; but he who destroys a good book kills reason itself, kills the image of God, as it were, in the eye.

JOHN MILTON

An ordinary man can . . . surround himself with two thousand books . . . and thenceforward have at least one place in the world in which it is possible to be happy.

AUGUSTINE BIRRELL

Only one hour in the normal day is more pleasurable than the hour spent in bed with a book before going to sleep, and that is the hour spent in bed with a book after being called in the morning.

ROSE MACAULAY

The pleasure of all reading is doubled when one lives with another who shares the same books.

KATHERINE MANSFIELD

Books are a delightful society. If you go into a room filled with books, even without taking them down from their shelves, they seem to speak to you, to welcome you.

WILLIAM E. GLADSTONE

There are books which I love to see on the shelf. I feel a virtue goes out of them, but I should think it undue familiarity to read them.

SAMUEL MC CHORD CROTHERS

Everywhere I have sought rest and found it not except sitting apart in a nook with a little book.

THOMAS KEMPIS

Just the knowledge that a good book is waiting one at the end of a long day makes that day happier.

KATHLEEN NORRIS

If you cannot read all your books, at any rate handle, or as it were, fondle them—peer into them, let them fall open where they will, read from the first sentence that arrests the eye, set them back on the shelves with your own hands, arrange them on your own plan so that you at least know where they are. Let them be your friends; let them at any rate be your acquaintances.

WINSTON CHURCHILL

Americans like fat books and thin women.

RUSSELL BAKER

I can't wait to run against a President who owns more tuxedos than books.

SENATOR GARY HART

In a very real sense, people who have read good literature have lived more than people who cannot or will not read. . . . It is not true that we have only one life to live; if we can read, we can live as many more lives and as many kinds of lives as we wish.

S.I. HAYAKAWA

It is a mistake to think that books have come to stay. The human race did without them for thousands of years and may decide to do without them again.

E.M. FORSTER

The world, you must remember, is only just becoming literate.

ALDOUS HUXLEY

This will never be a civilized country until we expend more money for books than we do for chewing gum.

ELBERT HUBBARD

The public which reads, in any sense of the word worth considering, is very, very small; the public which would feel no lack if all book-printing ceased tomorrow is enormous.

GEORGE GISSING

The man who does not read good books has no advantage over the man who can't read them.

MARK TWAIN

There's something special about people who are interested in the printed word. They are a species all their own— learned, kind, knowledgeable and human.

NATHAN PINE, *bookseller*

It is absurd to have a hard-and-fast rule about what one should read and what one shouldn't. More than half of modern culture depends on what one shouldn't read.

OSCAR WILDE

Books are fatal: they are the curse of the human race. Nine-tenths of existing books are nonsense, and the clever books are the refutation of that nonsense. The greatest misfortune that ever befell man was the invention of printing.

BENJAMIN DISRAELI

In literature, as in love, we are astonished at what is chosen by others.

ANDRE MAUROIS

Sir, the fact that a book is in the public library brings no comfort. Books are the one element in which I am personally and nakedly acquisitive. If it weren't for the law I would steal them. If it weren't for my purse I would buy them.

HAROLD LASKI

Never lend books, for no one ever returns them; the only books I have in my library are books that other folk have lent me.

ANATOLE FRANCE

Your borrowers of books—those mutilators of collections, spoilers of the symmetry of shelves, and creators of odd volumes.

CHARLES LAMB

When I get a little money, I buy books; and if any is left, I buy food and clothes.

DESIDERIUS ERASMUS

Hard-covered books break up friendships. You loan a hard-covered book to a friend and when he doesn't return it you get mad at him. It makes you mean and petty. But twenty-five cent books are different.

JOHN STEINBECK

The multitude of books is making us ignorant.

VOLTAIRE

There are times when I think that the reading I have done in the past has had no effect except to cloud my mind and make me indecisive.

ROBERTSON DAVIES

If we encounter a man of rare intellect, we should ask him what books he reads.

RALPH WALDO EMERSON

If I read a book that impresses me, I have to take myself firmly in hand before I mix with other people; otherwise they would think my mind rather queer.

ANNE FRANK

We live in an age that reads too much to be wise.

OSCAR WILDE

There is more treasure in books than in all the pirates' loot on Treasure Island . . . and best of all, you can enjoy these riches every day of your life.

WALT DISNEY

A book is like a garden carried in the pocket.
CHINESE PROVERB

Reading is to the mind what exercise is to the body.
SIR RICHARD STEELE

The best effect of any book is that it excites the reader to self-activity.
THOMAS CARLYLE

A man may as well expect to grow stronger by always eating as wiser by always reading.
JEREMY COLLIER

I would never read a book if it were possible for me to talk half an hour with the man who wrote it.
WOODROW WILSON

No woman was ever ruined by a book.
MAYOR JIMMY WALKER *of New York City*

Those whom books will hurt will not be proof against events. If some books are deemed more baneful and their sale forbid, how, then, with deadlier facts, not dreams of doting men? Events, not books, should be forbid.
HERMAN MELVILLE

There is a great deal of difference between an eager man who wants to read a book and a tired man who wants a book to read.
G.K. CHESTERTON

I divide all readers into two classes; those who read to remember and those who read to forget.

WILLIAM LYON PHELPS

As a rule reading fiction is as hard to me as trying to hit a target by hurling feathers at it. I need *resistance* to cerebrate!

WILLIAM JAMES

No man understands a deep book until he has seen and lived at least part of its contents.

EZRA POUND

A book is a mirror; if an ass peers into it, you can't expect an apostle to peer out.

GEORG CHRISTOPH LICHTENBERG

When you reread a classic you do not see more in the book than you did before; you see more in *you* than was there before.

CLIFTON FADIMAN

The art of reading is in great part that of acquiring a better understanding of life from one's encounter with it in a book.

ANDRE MAUROIS

I suggest that the only books that influence us are those for which we are ready, and which have gone a little farther down our particular path than we have yet gone ourselves.

E.M. FORSTER

There are some books one needs maturity to enjoy just as there are books an adult can come upon too late to savor.

PHYLLIS MC GINLEY

No book is really worth reading at the age of ten which is not equally (and often far more) worth reading at the age of fifty and beyond.

C.S. LEWIS

The stories of childhood leave an indelible impression, and their author always has a niche in the temple of memory from which the image is never cast out to be thrown on the rubbish heap of things that are outgrown and outlived.

HOWARD PYLE

The road to ignorance is paved with good editions.

GEORGE BERNARD SHAW

Every man who knows how to read has it in his power to magnify himself, to multiply the ways in which he exists, to make his life full, significant and interesting.

ALDOUS HUXLEY

When we read too fast or too slowly, we understand nothing.

BLAISE PASCAL

Who knows if Shakespeare might not have thought less if he had read more.

EDWARD YOUNG

The players often mention it as an honor to Shakespeare that in his writing, whatsoever he penned, he never blotted out a line. My answer hath been, "Would he had blotted a thousand."

BEN JONSON

I have not wasted my life trifling with literary fools in taverns as Jonson did when he should have been shaking England with the thunder of his spirit.

GEORGE BERNARD SHAW

Where is human nature so weak as in the bookstore?

HENRY WARD BEECHER

The oldest books are still only just out to those who have not read them.

SAMUEL BUTLER

The worst thing about new books is that they keep us from reading the old ones.

JOSEPH JOUBERT

Of course no writers ever forget their first acceptance. . . . One fine day when I was seventeen I had my first, second and third, all in the same morning's mail. Oh, I'm here to tell you, dizzy with excitement is no mere phrase!

TRUMAN CAPOTE

Publication—is the auction of the Mind of Man.

EMILY DICKINSON

There is a good saying to the effect that when a new book appears one should read an old one. As an author I would not recommend too strict an adherence to this saying.
    WINSTON CHURCHILL

One old lady who wants her head lifted wouldn't be so bad, but you multiply her two hundred and fifty thousand times and what you get is a book club.
    FLANNERY O'CONNOR

For several days after my first book was published I carried it about in my pocket, and took surreptitious peeps at it to make sure the ink had not faded.
    SIR JAMES M. BARRIE

I am very foolish over my own book. I have a copy which I constantly read and find very illuminating. Swift confesses to something of the sort with his own compositions.
    J.B. YEATS *in a letter to his son,* W.B. YEATS

I don't keep any copy of my books around. . . . They would embarrass me. When I finish writing my books, I kick them in the belly, and have done with them.
    LUDWIG BEMELMANS

If there is a special Hell for writers it would be in the forced contemplation of their own works, with all the misconceptions, the omissions, the failures that any finished work of art implies.
    JOHN DOS PASSOS

On the day when a young writer corrects his first proofsheet he is as proud as a schoolboy who has just gotten his first dose of the pox.

CHARLES BAUDELAIRE

Most of the basic material a writer works with is acquired before the age of fifteen.

WILLA CATHER

However great a man's natural talent may be, the art of writing cannot be learned all at once.

JEAN JACQUES ROUSSEAU

When I was twenty I was in love with words, a wordsmith. I didn't know enough to know when people were letting words get in their way. Now I like the words to disappear, like a transparent curtain.

WALLACE STEGNER

I have never been good at revising. I always thought I made things worse by recasting and retouching. I never knew what was meant by choice of words. It was one word or none.

ROBERT FROST

As for my next book, I am going to hold myself from writing it till I have it impending in me: grown heavy in my mind like a ripe pear; pendant, gravid, asking to be cut or it will fall.

VIRGINIA WOOLF

For a dyed-in-the-wool author nothing is as dead as a book once it is written. . . . She is rather like a cat whose kittens have grown-up. While they were a-growing she was passionately interested in them but now they seem hardly to belong to her—and probably she is involved with another batch of kittens as I am involved with other writing.

RUMER GODDEN

When I read my first book, I started writing my first book. I have never not been writing.

GORE VIDAL

Looking back, I imagine I was always writing. Twaddle it was too. But better far write twaddle or anything, anything, than nothing at all.

KATHERINE MANSFIELD

I suppose I am a born novelist, for the things I imagine are more vital and vivid to me than the things I remember.

ELLEN GLASGOW

If we should ever inaugurate a hall of fame, it would be reserved exclusively and hopefully for authors who, having written four bestsellers, *still refrained* from starting out on a lecture tour.

E.B. WHITE

A good title should be like a good metaphor: It should intrigue without being too baffling or too obvious.

WALKER PERCY

Almost all the great writers have as their *motif*, more or less disguised, the "passage from childhood to maturity," the clash between the thrill of expectation, and the disillusioning knowledge of the truth. *Lost Illusion* is the undisclosed title of every novel.

ANDRE MAUROIS

I'm terrible about titles; I don't know how to come up with them. They're the one thing in the story I'm really uncertain about.

EUDORA WELTY

Sometimes people give titles to me, and sometimes I see them on a billboard.

ROBERT PENN WARREN

There are some books of which scores of copies are bought for one which is read, and others which have dozens of readers for every copy sold.

JOHN AYSCOUGH

What a sense of superiority it gives one to escape reading a book which everyone else is reading.

ALICE JAMES

Some writers thrive with the contact with the commerce of success; others are corrupted by it. Perhaps, like losing one's virginity it is not as bad (or as good) as one feared it was going to be.

V.S. PRITCHETT

When I am dead, I hope it may be said:
"His sins were scarlet, but his books were read."
HILAIRE BELLOC

There are two motives for reading a book; one, that you enjoy it; the other, that you can boast about it.
BERTRAND RUSSELL

Best-Sellerism is the star system of the book world. A "best-seller" is a celebrity among books. It is known primarily (sometimes exclusively) for its well-knownness.
DANIEL J. BOORSTIN

There are books and there is literature. I have never met anyone who bought a book on the bestseller lists.
ELIZABETH HARDWICK

A best-seller is the gilded tomb of a mediocre talent.
LOGAN PEARSALL SMITH

I'm a lousy writer; a helluva lot of people have got lousy taste.
GRACE METALIOUS

Those big-shot writers . . . could never dig the fact that there are more salted peanuts consumed than caviar.
MICKEY SPILLANE

I try to leave out the parts that people skip.
ELMORE LEONARD

Bombario, the Hunchback, who was used as a
writing-desk by the brokers and who earned
£6000 in a few days.

Almost anyone can be an author; the business is to collect money and fame from this state of being.

A.A. MILNE

Writing is the only profession where no one considers you ridiculous if you earn no money.

JULES RENARD

Sir, no man but a blockhead ever wrote except for money.

SAMUEL JOHNSON

The profession of book-writing makes horse racing seem like a solid, stable business.

JOHN STEINBECK

If writers were good businessmen, they'd have too much sense to be writers.

IRVIN S. COBB

The multitude of books is a great evil. There is no measure or limit to this fever of writing; everyone must be an author, some for some kind of vanity to acquire celebrity and raise a name, others for the sake of lucre or gain.

MARTIN LUTHER

I do think that the quality which makes a man want to write and be read is essentially a desire for self-exposure and is masochistic. Like one of those guys who has a compulsion to take his thing out and show it on the street.

JAMES JONES

I don't want to take up literature in a money-making spirit, or be very anxious about making large profits, but selling it at a loss is another thing altogether, and an amusement I cannot well afford.

LEWIS CARROLL

Instead of marvelling with Johnson, how anything but profit should incite men to literary labour, I am rather surprised that mere emolument should induce them to labour so well.

THOMAS GREEN

One of the least impressive liberties is the liberty to starve. This particular liberty is freely accorded to authors.

LORD GOODMAN

Years ago, to say you were a writer was not the highest recommendation to your landlord. Today, he at least hesitates before he refuses to rent you an apartment—for all he knows you may be rich.

ARTHUR MILLER

When one says that a writer is fashionable one practically always means that he is admired by people under thirty.

GEORGE ORWELL

The secret of popular writing is never to put more on a given page than the common reader can lap off it with no strain *whatsoever* on his habitually slack attention.

EZRA POUND

An author is a person who can never take innocent pleasure in visiting a bookstore again. Say you go in and discover that there are no copies of your book on the shelves. You resent all the other books—I don't care if they are *Great Expectations, Life on the Mississippi,* and the *King James Bible*—that are on the shelves.

ROY BLOUNT, JR.

A man really writes for an audience of about ten persons. Of course, if others like it, that is clear gain. But if those ten are satisfied, he is content.

ALFRED NORTH WHITEHEAD

I write what I would like to read—what I think other women would like to read. If what I write makes a woman in the Canadian mountains cry and she writes and tells me about it, especially if she says "I read it to Tom when he came in from work and he cried too," I feel I have succeeded.

KATHLEEN NORRIS, *on the publication of her seventy-eighth book*

When I was a ten-year-old book worm and used to kiss the dust jacket pictures of authors as if they were icons, it used to amaze me that these remote people could provoke me to love.

ERICA JONG

Anything that is written to please the author is worthless.

BLAISE PASCAL

Any writer overwhelmingly honest about pleasing himself is almost sure to please others.

MARIANNE MOORE

My purpose is to entertain myself first and other people secondly.

JOHN D. MACDONALD

When I write, I aim in my mind not toward New York but toward a vague spot a little east of Kansas. I think of the books on library shelves, without their jackets, years old, and a countryish teen-aged boy finding them, and having them speak to him. The reviews, the stacks in Brentano's, are just hurdles to get over, to place the books on that shelf.

JOHN UPDIKE

A kid is a guy I never wrote down to. He's interested in what I say if I make it interesting. He is also the last container of a sense of humor, which disappears as he gets older, and he laughs only according to the way the boss, society, politics, or race want him to. Then he becomes an adult. And an adult is an obsolete child.

THEODORE GEISEL (Dr. Seuss)

The public and the reviewers have always given way, and always give way, to the idiosyncrasies of an author who is strong enough to make them. The history of literature is nothing but the performance of authors of feats which the best experience had declared could not be performed.

ARNOLD BENNETT

I do not believe the expenditure of $2.50 for a book entitles the purchaser to the personal friendship of the author.

EVELYN WAUGH

Writing is one of the few professions left where you take all the responsibility for what you do. It's really dangerous and ultimately destroys you as a writer if you start thinking about responses to your work or what your audience needs.

ERICA JONG

Writers, if they are worthy of that jealous designation, do not write for other writers. They write to give reality to experience.

ARCHIBALD MACLEISH

A man who writes well writes not as others write, but as he himself writes; it is often in speaking badly that he speaks well.

MONTESQUIEU

In a very real sense, the writer writes in order to teach himself, to understand himself, to satisfy himself; the publishing of his ideas, though it brings gratifications, is a curious anticlimax.

ALFRED KAZIN

Success comes to a writer, as a rule, so gradually that it is always something of a shock to him to look back and realize the heights to which he has climbed.

P.G. WODEHOUSE

America is about the last place in which life will be endurable at all for an inspired writer.

SAMUEL BUTLER

In America only the successful writer is important, in France all writers are important, in England no writer is important, in Australia you have to explain what a writer is.

GEOFFREY COTTERELL

A Frenchman can humiliate an Englishman just as readily as an Englishman can humiliate an American, and an American a Canadian. One of Canada's most serious literary needs is some lesser nation to domineer over and shame by displays of superior taste.

ROBERTSON DAVIES

Literature plays an important role in our country, helping the Party to educate the people correctly, to instill in them advanced, progressive ideas by which our Party is guided. And it is not without reason that writers in our country are called engineers of the human soul.

NIKITA KHRUSHCHEV

No wonder the really powerful men in our society, whether politicians or scientists, hold writers and poets in contempt. They do it because they get no evidence from modern literature that anybody is thinking about any significant question.

SAUL BELLOW

To write is to write is to write is to write is to write is to write is to write is to write.

GERTRUDE STEIN

Word has somehow got around that the split infinitive is always wrong. That is a piece with the outworn notion that it is always wrong to strike a lady.

JAMES THURBER

The difference between the right word and the nearly right word is the same as that between lightning and the lightning bug.

MARK TWAIN

You can be a little ungrammatical if you come from the right part of the country.

ROBERT FROST

I often think how much easier life would have been for me and how much time I would have saved if I had known the alphabet. I can never tell where *I* and *J* stand without saying *G, H* to myself first. I don't know whether *P* comes before *R* or after, and where *T* comes in has to this day remained something that I have never been able to get into my head.

W. SOMERSET MAUGHAM

Any writer worth the name is always getting into one thing or getting out of another thing.

FANNIE HURST

In conversation you can use timing, a look, inflection, pauses. But on the page all you have is commas, dashes, the amount of syllables in a word. When I write I read everything out loud to get the right rhythm.

FRAN LEBOWITZ

Writing is easy; all you do is sit staring at a blank sheet of paper until the drops of blood form on your forehead.

GENE FOWLER

When I hear about writer's block, this one and that one! f★★k off! Stop writing, for Christ's sake: Plenty more where you came from.

GORE VIDAL

I lost everything at Philippi, and took to poetry to make a living, but now I have a competence I should be mad if I did not prefer ease to writing.

HORACE

When I stepped from hard manual work to writing, I just stepped from one kind of hard work to another.

SEAN O'CASEY

Nothing you write, if you hope to be any good, will ever come out as you first hoped.

LILLIAN HELLMAN

I can't write five words but that I change seven.

DOROTHY PARKER

If you are getting the worst of it in an argument with a literary man, always attack his style. That'll touch him if nothing else will.

J.A. SPENDER

In stating as fully as I could how things really were, it was often very difficult and I wrote awkwardly and the awkwardness is what they called my style. All mistakes and awkwardness are easy to see, and they called it style.

ERNEST HEMINGWAY

I have written—often several times— every word I have ever published. My pencils outlast their erasures.

VLADIMIR NABOKOV

I quit writing if I feel inspired, because I know I'm going to have to throw it away. Writing a novel is like building a wall brick by brick; only amateurs believe in inspiration.

FRANK YERBY

. . . there are days when the result is so bad that no fewer than five revisions are required. In contrast, when I'm greatly inspired, only four revisions are needed.

JOHN KENNETH GALBRAITH

You will have to write and put away or burn a lot of material before you are comfortable in this medium. You might as well start now and get the necessary work done. For I believe that eventually quantity will make for quality.

RAY BRADBURY

I write a lot—every day, seven days a week—and I throw a lot away. Sometimes I think I write to throw away; it's a process of distillation.
DONALD BARTHELME

The wastepaper basket is the writer's best friend.
ISAAC B. SINGER

Read over your compositions and, when you meet a passage which you think is particularly fine, strike it out.
SAMUEL JOHNSON

To write simply is as difficult as to be good.
W. SOMERSET MAUGHAM

A bad book is as much a labor to write as a good one; it comes as sincerely from the author's soul.
ALDOUS HUXLEY

It takes less time to learn to write nobly than to learn to write lightly and straightforwardly.
FRIEDRICH WILHELM NIETZSCHE

All a writer has to do is get a woman to say he's a writer; it's an aphrodisiac.
SAUL BELLOW

Pretty women swarm around everybody but writers. Plain, intelligent women *somewhat* swarm around writers.
WILLIAM SAROYAN

If you were a member of Jesse James' band and people asked you what you were, you wouldn't say, 'Well, I'm a desperado.' You'd say something like 'I work in banks' or 'I've done some railroad work.' It took me a long time just to say 'I'm a writer.' It's really embarrassing.

ROY BLOUNT, JR.

Most writers are in a state of gloom a good deal of the time; they need perpetual reassurance.

JOHN HALL WHEELOCK

It's my experience that very few writers, young or old, are really seeking advice when they give out their work to be read. They want support; they want someone to say, 'Good job'. "

JOHN IRVING

Writing is not a profession but a vocation of unhappiness.

GEORGES SIMENON

Writing a book is not as tough as it is to haul 35 people around the country and sweat like a horse five nights a week.

BETTE MIDLER

For forty-odd years in this noble profession
I've harbored a guilt and my conscience is smitten.
So here is my slightly embarrassed confession—
I don't like to write, but I love to have written.

MICHAEL KANIN

I love being a writer. What I can't stand is the paperwork.

PETER DE VRIES

It is a fact that few novelists enjoy the creative labour, though most enjoy thinking about the creative labour.

ARNOLD BENNETT

What release to write so that one forgets oneself, forgets one's companion, forgets where one is or what one is going to do next—to be drenched in sleep or in the sea. Pencils and pads and curling blue sheets alive with letters heap up on the desk.

ANNE MORROW LINDBERGH

I am convinced that all writers are optimists whether they concede the point or not. . . . How otherwise could any human being sit down to a pile of blank sheets and decide to write, say two hundred thousand words on a given theme?

THOMAS COSTAIN

If we had to say what writing is, we would define it essentially as an act of courage.

CYNTHIA OZICK

Whatever our theme in writing, it is old and tried. Whatever our place, it has been visited by the stranger, it will never be new again. It is only the vision that can be new; but that is enough.

EUDORA WELTY

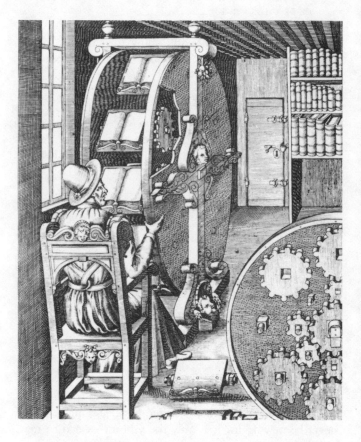

The writer, like the priest, must be exempted from secular labor. His work needs a frolic health; he must be at the top of his condition.

RALPH WALDO EMERSON

The writer has taken unto himself the former function of the priest or prophet. He presumes to order and legislate the people's life. There is no person more arrogant than the writer.

CORNELIUS REGISTER

Read, read, read. Read everything—trash, classics, good and bad, and see how they do it. Just like a carpenter who works as an apprentice and studies the master. Read! You'll absorb it. Then write. If it is good, you'll find out. If it's not, throw it out the window.

WILLIAM FAULKNER

It took me fifteen years to discover I had no talent for writing, but I couldn't give it up because by that time I was too famous.

ROBERT BENCHLEY

You must not suppose, because I am a man of letters, that I never tried to earn an honest living.

GEORGE BERNARD SHAW

An incurable itch for scribbling takes possession of many and grows inveterate in their insane hearts.

JUVENAL

Another damned thick, square book! Always scribble, scribble! Eh! Mr. Gibbon?

THE DUKE OF GLOUCESTER, *upon accepting the second volume of* A History of the Decline and Fall of the Roman Empire *from its author*

The devoted writer of humor must continue to try to come as close to the truth as he can, even if he gets burned in the process, but I don't think he will get too badly burned. His faith in the good will, the soundness, and the sense of humor of his countrymen will always serve as his asbestos curtain.

JAMES THURBER

It's much easier to write a solemn book than a funny book. It's harder to make people laugh than it is to make them cry. People are always on the verge of tears.

FRAN LEBOWITZ

Boozing does not necessarily have to go hand in hand with being a writer, as seems to be the concept in America. I therefore solemnly declare to all young men trying to become writers that they do not actually have to become drunkards first.

NELSON ALDRICH

Some American writers who have known each other for years have never met in the daytime or when both were sober.

JAMES THURBER

I wrote a short story because I wanted to see something of mine in print other than my fingers.
WILSON MIZNER

I put a piece of paper under my pillow, and when I could not sleep I wrote in the dark.
HENRY DAVID THOREAU

I put things down on sheets of paper and stuff them in my pockets. When I have enough, I have a book.
JOHN LENNON

Failure is very difficult for a writer to bear, but very few can manage the shock of early success.
MAURICE VALENCY

This is what I find encouraging about the writing trades: They allow mediocre people who are patient and industrious to revise their stupidity, to edit themselves into something like intelligence. They also allow lunatics to seem saner than sane.
KURT VONNEGUT, JR.

Some men borrow books; some men steal books; and others beg presentation copies from the author.
JAMES JEFFREY ROCHE

From the moment I picked your book up until I laid it down I was convulsed with laughter. Someday I intend reading it.
GROUCHO MARX, *on S.J. Perelman's first book*

It is the part of prudence to thank an author for his book before reading it, so as to avoid the necessity of lying about it afterwards.

GEORGE SANTAYANA

No one can write decently who is distrustful of the reader's intelligence, or whose attitude is patronizing.

E.B. WHITE

They always think that if you write well you're somehow cheating, you're not being democratic by writing as badly as everybody else does.

GORE VIDAL

If you want to get rich from writing, write the sort of thing that's read by persons who move their lips when they're reading to themselves.

DON MARQUIS

In my opinion the readers of novels are far more intelligent than unsuccessful writers will believe. They are expert in detecting and merciless to the conceited author, and the insincere author, and the author with all the tools of literature at his command who has nothing to say worth reading.

NEVIL SHUTE

Everything goes by the board: honor, pride, decency . . . to get the book written. If a writer has to rob his mother, he will not hesitate; the *Ode on a Grecian Urn* is worth any number of old ladies.

WILLIAM FAULKNER

The most essential gift for a good writer is a built-in shock-proof shit-detector.

ERNEST HEMINGWAY

Nature, not content with denying him the ability to think, has endowed him with the ability to write.

A.E. HOUSMAN

Writing is an adventure. To begin with, it is a toy and an amusement. Then it becomes a mistress, then it becomes a master, then it becomes a tyrant. The last phase is that just as you are about to be reconciled to your servitude, you kill the monster and fling him to the public.

WINSTON CHURCHILL

In literature today, there are plenty of masons but few good architects.

JOSEPH JOUBERT

Literature is an occupation in which you have to keep proving your talent to people who have none.

JULES RENARD

The difference between journalism and literature is that journalism is unreadable and literature is not read.

OSCAR WILDE

There's nothing to writing. All you do is sit down at a typewriter and open a vein.

RED SMITH

I think I did pretty well, considering I started out with nothing but a bunch of blank paper.
STEVE MARTIN

The machine has several virtues. . . . One may lean back in his chair and work it. It piles an awful stack of words on one page. It don't muss things or scatter ink blots around.
from MARK TWAIN'S *first letter written on a typewriter*

Sometimes I think it sounds like I walked out of the room and left the typewriter running.
GENE FOWLER

When a book, any sort of book, reaches a certain intensity of artistic performance it becomes literature. That intensity may be a matter of style, situation, character, emotional tone, or idea, or half a dozen other things. It may also be a perfection of control over the movement of a story similar to the control a great pitcher has over a ball.
RAYMOND CHANDLER

Poets are like baseball pitchers. Both have their moments. The intervals are the tough things.
ROBERT FROST

They can't yank a novelist like they can a pitcher. A novelist has to go the full nine, even if it kills him.
ERNEST HEMINGWAY

We romantic writers are there to make people feel and not think. A historical romance is the only kind of book where chastity really counts.

BARBARA CARTLAND

People do not deserve to have good writing, they are so pleased with bad.

RALPH WALDO EMERSON

To read a group of novels these days is a depressing experience. After the fourth or fifth, I find myself thinking about 'The Novel' and I feel a desperate desire to sneak out to a movie.

LESLIE FIEDLER

I think you must remember that a writer is a simple-minded person to begin with and go on that basis. He's not a great mind, he's not a great thinker, he's not a great philosopher, he's a storyteller.

ERSKINE CALDWELL

Immature artists imitate. Mature artists steal.

LIONEL TRILLING

When a thing has been said, and well said, have no scruple: take it and copy it.

ANATOLE FRANCE

Remember why the good Lord made your eyes,
Pla-gi-a-rize!

TOM LEHRER

If you copy from one author it's plagiarism. If you copy from two, it's research.

WILSON MIZNER

Next o'er his books his eyes began to roll,
In pleasing memory of all he stole.

ALEXANDER POPE

Just get it down on paper, and then we'll see what to do with it.

MAXWELL PERKINS' *advice to Marcia Davenport*

There are three rules for writing the novel. Unfortunately, no one knows what they are.

SOMERSET MAUGHAM

Never make excuses, never let them see you bleed, and never get separated from your baggage.

from WESLEY PRICE'S *"Three Rules of Professional Comportment for Writers"*

Writing is for the most part a lonely and unsatisfying occupation. One is tied to a table, a chair, a stack of paper.

GRAHAM GREENE

When I am working on a book or a story I write every morning as soon after the first light as possible. There is no one to disturb you and it is cool or cold and you come to your work and warm as you write.

ERNEST HEMINGWAY

The tools I need for my work are paper, tobacco, food, and a little whisky.

WILLIAM FAULKNER

The ideal view for daily writing, hour on hour, is the blank brick wall of a cold-storage warehouse. Failing this, a stretch of sky will do, cloudless if possible.

EDNA FERBER

The perfect place for a writer is in the hideous roar of a city, with men making a new road under his window in competition with a barrel organ, and on the mat a man waiting for the rent.

HENRY VOLLAM MORTON

Writing is a solitary occupation. Family, friends, and society are the natural enemies of a writer. He must be alone, uninterrupted, and slightly savage if he is to sustain and complete an undertaking.

LAWRENCE CLARK POWELL

I felt like you can write forever, but you have a short time to raise a family. And I think a family is a lot more important than writing.

KEN KESEY

All my major works have been written in prison. . . . I would recommend prison not only to aspiring writers but to aspiring politicians, too.

JAWAHARLAL NEHRU

GOLD AND SILVER PENCILS. (Hall Marked.)

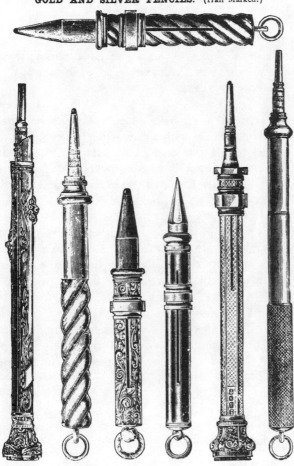

The best time for planning a book is while you're doing the dishes.

AGATHA CHRISTIE

What no wife of a writer can ever understand is that a writer is working when he's staring out of the window.

BURTON RASCOE

Often while reading a book one feels that the author would have preferred to paint rather than write; one can sense the pleasure he derives from describing a landscape or a person, as if he were painting what he is saying, because deep in his heart he would have preferred to use brushes and colors.

PABLO PICASSO

Writing is a form of therapy; sometimes I wonder how all those who do not write, compose or paint can manage to escape the madness, the melancholia, the panic fear which is inherent in a human situation.

GRAHAM GREENE

The man of letters loves not only to be read but to be seen. Happy to be by himself, he would be happier still if people knew that he was happy to be by himself, working in solitude at night under his lamp.

REMY DE GOURMONT

If I could I would always work in silence and obscurity, and let my efforts be known by their results.

EMILY BRONTË

Only ambitious nonentities and hearty mediocrities exhibit their rough drafts. It is like passing around samples of one's sputum.

VLADIMIR NABOKOV

I just think it's bad to talk about one's present work, for it spoils something at the root of the creative act. It discharges the tension.

NORMAN MAILER

Mostly, we authors must repeat ourselves—that's the truth. We have two or three great moving experiences in our lives—experiences so great and moving that it doesn't seem at the time that anyone else has been caught up and pounded and dazzled and astonished and beaten and broken and rescued and illuminated and rewarded and humbled in just that way ever before.

F. SCOTT FITZGERALD

I think that in order to write really well and convincingly, one must be somewhat poisoned by emotion. Dislike, displeasure, resentment, fault-finding, imagination, passionate remonstrance, a sense of injustice—they all make fine fuel.

EDNA FERBER

I wrote the scenes . . . by using the same apprehensive imagination that occurs in the morning before an afternoon's appointment with my dentist.

JOHN MARQUAND

I've always believed in writing without a collaborator, because where two people are writing the same book, each believes he gets all the worries and only half the royalties.

AGATHA CHRISTIE

I never could understand how two men can write a book together; to me that's like three people getting together to have a baby.

EVELYN WAUGH

Why do people always expect authors to answer questions? I am an author because I want to *ask* questions. If I had answers I'd be a politician.

EUGENE IONESCO

INTERVIEWER: *How many drafts of a story do you do?*
S.J. PERELMAN: Thirty-seven. I once tried doing thirty-three, but something was lacking, a certain—how shall I say?—*je ne sais quoi.* On another occasion, I tried forty-two versions, but the final effect was too lapidary—you know what I mean, Jack? What the hell are you trying to extort—my trade secrets?

People who read me seem to be divided into four groups: twenty-five percent like me for the right reasons; twenty-five percent like me for the wrong reasons; twenty-five percent hate me for the wrong reasons; twenty-five percent hate me for the right reasons. It's that last twenty-five percent that worries me.

ROBERT FROST

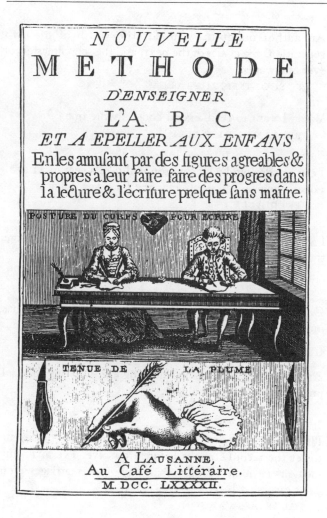

NOUVELLE

METHODE

D'ENSEIGNER

L'A. B C

ET A EPELLER AUX ENFANS

En les amuſant par des figures agreables &
propres à leur faire faire des progres dans
la leĉure & l'écriture preſque ſans maître.

POSTURE DU CORPS ... POUR ECRIRE

TENUE DE LA PLUME

A LAUSANNE,
Au Café Littéraire.
M. DCC. LXXXXII.

An author ought to write for the youth of his own generation, the critics of the next, and the schoolmasters of ever afterwards.

F. SCOTT FITZGERALD

When I want to read a good book, I write one.

BENJAMIN DISRAELI

I can't understand why a person will take a year to write a novel when he can easily buy one for a few dollars.

FRED ALLEN

I never desire to converse with a man who has written more than he has read.

SAMUEL JOHNSON

Only when one has lost all curiosity about the future has one reached the age to write an autobiography.

EVELYN WAUGH

And because I found I had nothing else to write about, I presented myself as a subject.

MONTAIGNE

I'll be eighty this month. Age, if nothing else, entitles me to set the record straight before I dissolve. I've given my memoirs far more thought than any of my marriages. You can't divorce a book.

GLORIA SWANSON

A well-written life is almost as rare as a well-spent one.
THOMAS CARLYLE

The man who writes about himself and his own time is the only man who writes about all people and about all time.
GEORGE BERNARD SHAW

How can one make a life out of six cardboard boxes full of tailors' bills, love letters and old picture postcards?
VIRGINIA WOOLF

A novelist, in his omniscience, knows the measure of his characters, out of his passion for all sorts of conditions of human life. The biographer, however, begins with certain limiting little facts.
LEON EDEL

On the trail of another man, the biographer must put up with finding himself at every turn: any biography uneasily shelters an autobiography within it.
PAUL MURRAY KENDALL

The novel is the highest example of subtle interrelatedness that man has discovered.
D.H. LAWRENCE

As a fiction writer I find it convenient not to believe things. Not to disbelieve them either, just move them into a realm where everything is held in suspension.
WILLIAM GASS

What makes a good writer of history is a guy who is suspicious. Suspicion marks the real difference between the man who wants to write honest history and the one who'd rather write a good story.

JIM BISHOP

People need books with an epic background. They are bored with books that tell only one story on one level. They need something fantastic, something that gives them a sense of living in history. As it is, most novels aren't giving readers a chance to use their sense of history.

GÜNTER GRASS

Everyone who works in the domain of fiction is a bit crazy. The problem is to render this craziness interesting.

FRANCOIS TRUFFAUT

Every author really wants to have letters printed in the papers. Unable to make the grade, he drops down a rung of the ladder and writes novels.

P.G. WODEHOUSE

I have never met an author who admitted that people did not buy his book because it was dull.

W. SOMERSET MAUGHAM

Prose books are the show dogs I breed and sell to support my cat.

ROBERT GRAVES, *on writing novels to support his love of writing poetry*

Writing is a dog's life, but the only life worth living.
GUSTAVE FLAUBERT

The value of great fiction, we begin to suspect, is not that it entertains us or distracts us from our troubles, not just that it broadens our knowledge of people and places, but also that it helps us to know what we believe, reinforces the qualities that are noblest in us, leads us to feel uneasy about our failures and limitations.
JOHN GARDNER

When audiences come to see us authors lecture, it is largely in the hope that we'll be funnier to look at than to read.
SINCLAIR LEWIS

A writer's problem does not change. He himself changes and the world he lives in changes, but his problem remains the same. It is always how to write truly and, having found out what is true, to project it in such a way that it becomes a part of the experience of the person who reads it.
ERNEST HEMINGWAY

A writer is congenitally unable to tell the truth and that is why we call what he writes fiction.
WILLIAM FAULKNER

How pleasant it is to respect people! When I see books, I am not concerned with how the authors loved or played cards; I see only their marvellous works.
ANTON CHEKHOV

Writers seldom choose as friends those self-contained characters who are never in trouble, never unhappy or ill, never make mistakes, and always count their change when it is handed to them.

CATHERINE DRINKER BOWEN

There is only one trait that marks the writer. He is always watching. It's a kind of trick of the mind and he is born with it.

MORLEY CALLAGHAN

When you're a writer, you no longer see things with the freshness of the normal person. There are always two figures that work inside you, and if you are at all intelligent you realize that you have lost something. But I think there has always been this dichotomy in a real writer. He wants to be terribly human, and he responds emotionally, and at the same time there's this cold observer who cannot cry.

BRIAN MOORE

No tears in the writer, no tears in the reader. No surprise for the writer, no surprise for the reader.

ROBERT FROST

In any work that is truly creative, I believe, the writer cannot be omniscient in advance about the effects that he proposes to produce. The suspense of a novel is not only in the reader, but in the novelist, who is intensely curious about what will happen to the hero.

MARY MC CARTHY

How can you write if you can't cry?

RING LARDNER

Writing a book is a horrible, exhausting struggle, like a long bout of some painful illness. One would never undertake such a thing if one were not driven by some demon whom one can neither resist nor understand. For all one knows that demon is simply the same instinct that makes a baby squall for attention. And yet it is also true that one can write nothing readable unless one constantly struggles to efface one's personality. Good prose is like a windowpane.

GEORGE ORWELL

They're fancy talkers about themselves, writers. If I had to give young writers advice, I would say don't listen to writers talk about writing or themselves.

LILLIAN HELLMAN

Advice to young writers? Always the same advice: learn to trust your own judgement, learn inner independence, learn to trust that time will sort the good from the bad—including your own bad.

DORIS LESSING

Most writers, you know, are awful sticks to talk with.

SHERWOOD ANDERSON

All writers are vain, selfish, and lazy, and at the very bottom of their motives there lies a mystery.

GEORGE ORWELL

Writers seldom wish other writers well.

SAUL BELLOW

What a heartbreaking job it is trying to combine authors for their own protection! I had ten years of it on the Committee of Management of the Society of Authors; and the first lesson I learned was that when you take the field for the authors you will be safer without a breastplate than without a backplate.

GEORGE BERNARD SHAW

If I didn't know the ending of a story, I wouldn't begin. I always write my last line, my last paragraph, my last page first.

KATHERINE ANNE PORTER

Writing every book is like a purge; at the end of it one is empty . . . like a dry shell on the beach, waiting for the tide to come in again.

DAPHNE DU MAURIER

We need not worry much about writers. Man will always find a means to gratify a passion. He will write, as he commits adultery, in spite of taxation.

GRAHAM GREENE

I can always find plenty of women to sleep with but the kind of woman that is really hard for me to find is a typist who can read my writing.

THOMAS WOLFE

One hates an author that's all author.

LORD BYRON

Your manuscript is both good and original; but the part that is good is not original, and the part that is original is not good.

SAMUEL JOHNSON

Whenever you feel an impulse to perpetrate a piece of exceptionally fine writing, obey it . . . and delete it before sending your manuscript to the press.

SIR ARTHUR QUILLER-COUCH

Manuscript: something submitted in haste and returned at leisure.

OLIVER HERFORD

I've never signed a contract, so never have a deadline. A deadline's an unnerving thing. I just finish a book, and if the publisher doesn't like it that's his privilege. There've been many, many rejections. If you want to write it your own way, that's the chance you take.

MARCHETTE CHUTE

Never submit an idea or chapter to an editor or publisher, no matter how much he would like you to. Writing from the approved idea is (another) gravely serious time-waster. This is your story. Try and find out what your editor wants in advance, but then try and give it to him in one piece.

JOHN CREASEY

We have read your manuscript with boundless delight. If we were to publish your paper, it would be impossible for us to publish any work of lower standard. And as it is unthinkable that in the next thousand years we shall see its equal, we are, to our regret, compelled to return your divine composition, and to beg you a thousand times to overlook our short sight and timidity.

Rejection slip from a Chinese economic journal, quoted in the Financial Times.

The first thing an unpublished author should remember is that no one asked him to write in the first place. With this firmly in mind, he has no right to become discouraged just because other people are being published.

JOHN FARRAR

Only a small minority of authors over-write themselves. Most of the good and the tolerable ones do not write enough.

ARNOLD BENNETT

The faster I write the better my output. If I'm going slow I'm in trouble. It means I'm pushing the words instead of being pulled by them.

RAYMOND CHANDLER

With sixty staring me in the face, I have developed inflammation of the sentence structure and a definite hardening of the paragraphs.

JAMES THURBER, *at age 59*

A collection of short stories is generally thought to be a horrendous clinker; an enforced courtesy for the elderly writer who wants to display the trophies of his youth, along with his trout flies.

JOHN CHEEVER

I finished my first book seventy-six years ago. I offered it to every publisher on the English-speaking earth I had ever heard of. Their refusals were unanimous: and it did not get into print until, fifty years later, publishers would publish anything that had my name on it.

GEORGE BERNARD SHAW

Literary success of any enduring kind is made by refusing to do what publishers want, by refusing to write what the public wants, by refusing to accept any popular standard, by refusing to write anything to order.

LAFCADIO HEARN

A book must be done according to the writer's conception of it as nearly perfect as possible, and the publishing problems begin then. That is, the publisher must not try to get a writer to fit the book to the conditions of the trade, etc. It must be the other way around.

MAXWELL PERKINS

At least half the mystery novels published violate the law that the solution, once revealed, must seem to be inevitable.

RAYMOND CHANDLER

In the march up the heights of fame there comes a spot close to the summit in which man reads nothing but detective stories.

HEYWOOD HALE BROUN

The beginner who submits a detective novel longer than 80,000 words is courting rejection.

HOWARD HAYCRAFT

The detective himself should never turn out to be the culprit.

S.S. VAN DINE

Love interest nearly always weakens a mystery because it introduces a type of suspense that is antagonistic to the detective's struggle to solve a problem.

RAYMOND CHANDLER

The mystery story is two stories in one: the story of what happened and the story of what appeared to happen.

MARY ROBERTS RINEHART

There certainly does seem a possibility that the detective story will come to an end, simply because the public will have learnt all the tricks.

DOROTHY SAYERS

Science fiction stories are whatever science fiction editors buy.

JOHN CAMPBELL

A good science fiction story is a story with a human problem, and a human solution, which would not have happened without its science content.

THEODORE STURGEON

I love you sons of bitches. You're the only ones with guts enough to *really* care about the future, who *really* notice what machines do to us, what wars do to us, what cities do to us, what tremendous misunderstandings, mistakes, accidents, and catastrophes do to us. You're the only ones zany enough to agonize over time and distances without limit, over mysteries that will never die, over the fact that we are right now determining whether the space voyage for the next billion years or so is going to be Heaven or Hell.

The drunken hero of KURT VONNEGUT'S God
Bless You, Mr. Rosewater, *who blunders into a convention of science fiction writers*

You don't have to suffer to be a poet. Adolescence is enough suffering for anyone.

JOHN CIARDI

The poet, as everyone knows, must strike his individual note sometime between the ages of fifteen and twenty-five. He may hold it a long time, or a short time, but it is then he must strike it or never. School and college have been conducted with the almost express purpose of keeping him busy with something else till the danger of his ever creating anything has past.

ROBERT FROST

The crown of literature is poetry. It is its end and aim. It is the sublimest activity of the human mind. It is the achievement of beauty and delicacy. The writer of prose can only step aside when the poet passes.

W. SOMERSET MAUGHAM

Everybody has their own idea of what's a poet. Robert Frost, President Johnson, T.S. Eliot, Rudolf Valentino—they're all poets. I like to think of myself as the one who carries the light bulb.

BOB DYLAN

When power leads man to arrogance, poetry reminds him of his limitations. When power narrows the area of man's concern, poetry reminds him of the richness and diversity of his existence. When power corrupts, poetry cleanses.

PRESIDENT JOHN KENNEDY, *October 26, 1963 at the dedication of the Robert Frost Library, Amherst College*

Women have always been poor, not for two hundred years merely, but from the beginning of time . . . Women, then, have not had a dog's chance of writing poetry. That is why I have laid so much stress on money and a room of one's own.

VIRGINIA WOOLF

Modern poets talk against business, poor things, but all of us write for money. Beginners are subjected to trial by market, poor things.

ROBERT FROST

Poets aren't very useful.
Because they aren't consumeful or very produceful.
    OGDEN NASH

Like a piece of ice on a hot stove the poem must ride on its own melting.
    ROBERT FROST

Publishing a volume of verse is like dropping a rose-petal down the Grand Canyon and waiting for the echo.
    DON MARQUIS

Not gods, nor men, nor even booksellers have put up with poets being second-rate.
    HORACE

I've had it with these cheap sons of bitches who claim they love poetry but never buy a book.
    KENNETH REXROTH

Modesty is a virtue not often found among poets, for almost every one of them thinks himself the greatest in the world.
    MIGUEL DE CERVANTES

It's silly to suggest the writing of poetry as something ethereal, a sort of soul-crashing emotional experience that wrings you. I have no fancy ideas about poetry. It doesn't come to you on the wings of a dove. It's something you work hard at.
    LOUISE BOGAN

It is always hard for poets to believe that one says their poems are bad not because one is a fiend but because their poems are bad.

RANDALL JARRELL

Respect the children of the poor—from them come most poets.

MENDELE MOCHER SFORIM

Great poetry is always written by somebody straining to go beyond what he can do.

STEPHEN SPENDER

I went for years not finishing anything. Because, of course, when you finish something you can be judged. . . . I had poems which were re-written so many times I suspect it was just a way of avoiding sending them out.

ERICA JONG

A poem is never a put-up job so to speak. It begins as a lump in the throat, a sense of wrong, a homesickness, a love sickness. It is never a thought to begin with.

ROBERT FROST

To have written one good poem—*good* used seriously—is an unlikely and marvelous thing that only a couple hundred of writers of English, at the most, have done—it's like sitting out in the yard in the evening and having a meteorite fall in one's lap.

RANDALL JARRELL

If I feel physically as if the top of my head were taken off, I know that is poetry.

EMILY DICKINSON

I was too slow a mover. It was much easier to be a poet.

T.S. ELIOT *on giving up boxing in college*

I could no more define poetry than a terrier can define a rat.

A.E. HOUSMAN

I believe that every English poet should read the English classics, master the rules of grammar before he attempts to bend or break them, travel abroad, experience the horrors of sordid passion, and—if he is lucky enough—know the love of an honest woman.

ROBERT GRAVES

Were poets to be suppressed, my friends, with no history, no ancient lays, save that each had a father, nothing of any man would be heard hereafter.

GIOLLA BRIGHDE MHAC CON MIDH *(circa 1259)*

There are three things, after all, that a poem must reach: the eye, the ear, and what we may call the heart or the mind. It is most important of all to reach the heart of the reader.

ROBERT FROST

Let every eye negotiate for itself, and trust no agent.

WILLIAM SHAKESPEARE

A good writer is not, per se, a good book critic. No more than a good drunk is automatically a good bartender.

JIM BISHOP

I regard reviews as a kind of infant's disease to which new-born books are subject.

GEORG CHRISTOPH LICHTENBERG

A unanimous chorus of approval is not an assurance of survival; authors who please everyone at once are quickly exhausted.

ANDRÉ GIDE

Book reviewers have probably done more to kill the hard cover book trade than all the other evils, with which it is beset, combined. They almost invariably attack the best sellers, cutting down the astronomical totals to which these might soar, with which publishers try to recoup—what they lost on literary stuff that gets good reviews but small sales.

JACK WOODFORD

One thing I learned about my first novel was what all the reviewers thought of it, from Little Rock to Broken Hill, for I subscribed to a press-cutting agency, a thing I have not done since. I learned thus, what I have had no occasion to unlearn, that reviewers do not read books with much care, and that their profession is more given to stupidity and malice and literary ignorance even than the profession of novelist.

ANTHONY BURGESS

Insects sting, not in malice, but because they want to live.
It is the same with critics; they desire our blood, not our
pain.

FRIEDRICH NIETZSCHE

It's surprising that authors should expect kindness to be
shown to their books when they are not themselves known
for kindness toward their characters, their culture or by
implication their readers.

ANATOLE BROYARD

A perfect judge will read each work of wit.
With the same spirit that its author writ.

ALEXANDER POPE

Some reviews give pain. That is regrettable, but no author
has the right to whine. He was not obliged to be an author.
He invited publicity, and he must take the publicity that
comes along.

E.M. FORSTER

It is advantageous to an author that his book should be
attacked as well as praised. Fame is a shuttlecock. If it be
struck at only one end of the room, it will soon fall to the
ground. To keep it up, it must be struck at both ends.

SAMUEL JOHNSON

Nature fits all her children with something to do;
He who would write and can't write, can surely review.

JAMES RUSSELL LOWELL

It is as hard to find a neutral critic as it is a neutral country in time of war. I suppose if a critic were neutral, he wouldn't trouble to write anything.

KATHERINE ANNE PORTER

A serious reviewer should have an ax to grind. If you don't, your judgements will appear ephemeral, casual, even indifferent. But when you have an ax to grind, it is essential that you should not know what it is, and neither should anyone else.

ANATOLE BROYARD

I am sitting in the smallest room in my house. I have your review in front of me. Soon it will be behind me.

German composer MAX REGER

"Was it Eliot's toilet I saw?"
    Palindrome allegedly uttered by an American publisher
    after paying his first visit to the London firm of Faber
    and Faber

A person who publishes a book willfully appears before the populace with his pants down. . . . If it is a good book nothing can hurt him. If it is a bad book, nothing can help him.

EDNA ST. VINCENT MILLAY

It is safer to assume that every writer has read every word of every review, and will never forgive you.

JOHN LEONARD

When a man publishes a book, there are so many stupid things said that he declares he'll never do it again. The praise is almost always worse than the criticism.

SHERWOOD ANDERSON

I have long felt that any reviewer who expresses rage and loathing for a novel is preposterous. He or she is like a person who has put on full armor and attacked a hot fudge sundae or a banana split.

KURT VONNEGUT, JR.

Confronted by an absolutely infuriating review it is sometimes helpful for the victim to do a little personal research on the critic. Is there any truth to the rumor that he had no formal education beyond the age of eleven? In any event, is he able to construct a simple English sentence? Do his participles dangle? When moved to lyricism does he write "I had a fun time"? Was he ever arrested for burglary? I don't know that you will prove anything this way, but it is perfectly harmless and quite soothing.

JEAN KERR

An author who gives a manager or publisher any rights in his work except those immediately and specifically required for its publication or performance is for business purposes an imbecile. As 99 per cent of English authors and 100 per cent of American ones are just such imbeciles, managers and publishers make a practice of asking for every right the author possesses.

GEORGE BERNARD SHAW

I am absolutely convinced that every author of large and varied output ought to put the whole of his affairs into the hands of a good agent, and that every such author who fails to do so loses money by his omission.

ARNOLD BENNETT

In the past I was not so wise as I am now; I left nearly all my business to an agent. I am still encumbered with his slovenly and disadvantageous agreements.

H.G. WELLS

Writers hop from publisher to publisher mainly because of the size of the dollar, and their loyalty tends to be more toward the agent than either the publisher or editor.

SCOTT MEREDITH

Dick was a superb salesman, and the very fact that he hadn't read the books made him able to sell them that much better. Some of the best Hollywood agents, for instance, are the same. They can sell movie rights for much more when they haven't read a book than if they have.

BENNETT CERF

An editor should tell the author his writing is better than it is. Not a lot better, a little better.

T.S. ELIOT

Editors are extremely fallible people, all of them. Don't put too much trust in them.

MAXWELL PERKINS

The job of editor in a publishing house is the dullest, hardest, most exciting, exasperating and rewarding of perhaps any job in the world.

JOHN HALL WHEELOCK

Most editors generally can't recognize bad writing when they read it. Nor do they try very hard to learn to recognize it.

ALFRED KNOPF

Listen carefully to first criticisms of your work. Note just what it is about your work that the critics don't like—then cultivate it. That's the part of your work that's individual and worth keeping.

JEAN COCTEAU

Nine out of ten writers, I am sure, could write more. I think they should and, if they did, they would find their work improving even beyond their own, their agent's and their editor's highest hopes.

JOHN CREASEY

No passion in the world is equal to the passion to alter someone else's draft.

H.G. WELLS

Great editors do not discover nor produce great authors; great authors create and produce great publishers.

JOHN FARRAR

Editors at work

The average editor cannot escape feeling that telling a writer to do something is almost the same thing as performing it himself.

HEYWOOD CAMPBELL BROUN

Writing for the magazines sounds like a delightful occupation, but literally it means nothing without the cooperation of the editors of the magazines, and it is this cooperation which is difficult to secure.

A.A. MILNE

Each book, before the contract, is beautiful to contemplate. By the middle of the writing, the book has become, for the author, a hate object. For the editor, in the middle of editing, it has become a two-ton concrete necklace. However, both author and editor will recover the gleam in their eyes when the work is complete, and see the book as the masterwork it really is.

SAM VAUGHAN

Don't forget, both you and the editor are putting on an unceasing act for the public, and between you there should be the same relation that exists between the magician and his assistant, offstage.

JACK WOODFORD

Never buy an editor or publisher a lunch or a drink until he has bought an article, story or book from you. This rule is absolute and may be broken only at your peril.

JOHN CREASEY

Calvin Trillin once proposed that "the advance for a book should be at least as much as the cost of the lunch at which it was discussed." When he asked an editor what he thought of this formula, he was told that it was "unrealistic."

WILLARD ESPY

The writer who can't do his job looks to his editor to do it for him, though he wouldn't dream of offering to share his royalties with that editor.

ALFRED KNOPF

The truth is that editing lines is not necessarily the same as editing a book. A book is a much more complicated entity and totality than the sum of its lines alone. Its structural integrity, the relation and proportions of its parts, and its total impact could escape even a conscientious editor exclusively intent on vetting the book line by line.

BOB GOTTLIEB

I have performed the necessary butchery. Here is the bleeding corpse.

HENRY JAMES, *following a request from the* TLS *to cut three lines from a 5,000 word article.*

Everyone needs an editor.

TIM FOOTE *commenting in* Time *magazine upon the fact that Hitler's original title for* Mein Kampf *was* Four-and-a-Half Years of Struggle against Lies, Stupidity, and Cowardice

You know how it is in the kid's book world: It's just bunny eat bunny.

ANONYMOUS

One should fight like the devil the temptation to think well of editors. They are all, without exception—at least some of the time—incompetent or crazy. By the nature of their profession they read too much, with the result they grow jaded and cannot recognize talent though it dances in front of their eyes.

JOHN GARDNER

It circulated for five years, through the halls of fifteen publishers, and finally ended up with Vanguard Press, which, as you can see, is rather deep into the alphabet.

PATRICK DENNIS *commenting on* Auntie Mame

Editors are no longer father-confessors. Most of them are acquisition editors who are more concerned with bringing home the bacon than in trying to rewrite the bacon.

SCOTT MEREDITH

The greatest obstacle to good book publishing is the editorial board. One seasoned editor's judgement is of greater value than a committee of six.

WILLIAM TARG

A competent editor is a publisher in microcosm, able to initiate and follow a project all the way through.

MARC JAFFE

The one thing I have learned about editing over the years is that you have to edit and publish out of your own tastes, enthusiasms, and concerns, and not out of notions or guesswork about what other people might like to read.

NORMAN COUSINS

Then, in the end, you have your editor go out for himself as the publisher, on the basis of certain resolutions. One of these, is to my mind, a complete betrayal of his profession—that he will only publish books which will coincide with his own views.

MAXWELL PERKINS

You ask for the distinction between the terms "Editor" and "Publisher": an editor selects manuscripts; a publisher selects editors.

M. LINCOLN SCHUSTER

No, no, there must be a limit to the baseness even of publishers.

DOROTHY SAYERS

Publishers are all cohorts of the devil; there must be a special hell for them somewhere.

GOETHE

As repressed sadists are supposed to become policemen or butchers, so those with irrational fear of life become publishers.

CYRIL CONNOLLY

Gone today, here tomorrow.
    ALFRED KNOPF *on book returns*

At a London cocktail party, a woman came up to publisher Jonathan Cape and asked, 'Do you keep a copy of every book you print?' He replied, 'Madam, I keep thousands.'

I do not think publishing at all creditable either to men or women, and (though you will not believe me) very often feel ashamed of it myself.
    BYRON, *in a letter to Lady Carol Lamb*

I do not think publishing is hard work. I like publishing because it is possible to survive one's mistakes.
    MICHAEL JOSEPH

There are men that will make you books and turn 'em loose into the world with as much dispatch as they would do a dish of fritters.
    MIGUEL DE CERVANTES

People feel no obligation to buy books. It isn't their fault. Art seems cheap to them, because almost always it is cheap. . . . People stick any kind of stuff together between covers and throw it at them.
    SHERWOOD ANDERSON

On the whole, it is a flat time, and publishers have nothing to say to poets, regarding them as unprofitable people.
    SIR HENRY TAYLOR (*1800–1886*)

Most authors are born to be failures, and the publisher knows it. He makes his living out of the few successes, and if he is indulgent with less successful writers, it is not only because there is always the possibility that today's failure may become tomorrow's best-seller. Unless he has a genuine sympathy with the author's problems, no one can hope to make an enduring success of publishing.

MICHAEL JOSEPH

The balance sheets of our great publishing houses would not be materially affected if they ceased from tomorrow the publication of poetry and literary criticism, and most publishers would rejoice to be relieved of the unprofitable burden of vain solicitations which such publication encourages.

HERBERT READ

The fact is that the intrinsic worth of the book, play or whatever the author is trying to sell is the least, last factor in the whole transaction. There is probably no other trade in which there is so little relationship between profits and actual value, or into which sheer chance so largely enters.

GEORGE BERNARD SHAW

I draw up my own agreements with Messrs MacMillan, who also, as a matter of courtesy—and subject, of course, to a considerable use of the privilege—give me unlimited free copies. If any author is really worth publishing, he can get these terms from any decent publishing house.

H.G. WELLS

Until the manuscript is delivered, power is shared. When the manuscript enters the publishing process, power shifts to the publisher. It is the publisher who decides how the book is presented to the public.

TED SOLOTAROFF

Publishers will tell you, with their tongue in their cheek, the every manuscript which reaches their office is faithfully read, but they are not to be believed. At least fifteen out of twenty manuscripts can be summarily rejected, usually with safety. There may be a masterpiece among them, but it is a thousand to one against.

MICHAEL JOSEPH

Another illusion, seldom entertained by competent authors, is that the publisher's readers and others are waiting to plagiarize their work. I think it may be said that the more worthless the manuscript, the greater the fear of plagiarism.

STANLEY UNWIN

The publisher is a middleman, he calls the tune to which the whole of the rest of the trade dances; and he does so because he pays the piper.

GEOFFREY FABER

Publishing is a very mysterious business. It is hard to predict what kind of sale or reception a book will have, and advertising seems to do very little good.

THOMAS WOLFE *in a letter to his mother*

A small press is an attitude, a kind of anti-commerciality. The dollars come second, the talent and the quality of the writing come first. If the presses wanted to make money, they'd be out there selling cookbooks.

BILL HENDERSON

To write books is easy, it requires only pen and ink and the ever-patient paper. To print books is a little more difficult, because genius so often rejoices in illegible handwriting. To read books is more difficult still, because of the tendency to go to sleep. But the most difficult task of all that a mortal man can embark on is to sell a book.

from a poem by FELIX DAHN *paraphrased by*
SIR STANLEY UNWIN

Anyone can sell. The secret is to have 50,000 books in your basement.

MARY ELLEN PINKHAM

I should be sorry to think it was the publishers themselves that got up this entire little flutter to enable them to unload a book that was taking too much room in their cellars, but you can never tell what a publisher will do. I have been one myself.

MARK TWAIN, *when* Huck Finn *was banned in Omaha.*

They just wanted to sell *books*, that's all they wanted to do. It wasn't about anything, and I knew that—I figured they *had* to know that, they were in the business of it.

BOB DYLAN

I object to publishers: the one service they have done me is to teach me to do without them. They combine commercial rascality with artistic touchiness and pettishness, without being either good business men or fine judges of literature. All that is necessary in their production of a book is an author and a bookseller, without the intermediate parasite.

GEORGE BERNARD SHAW

Publishers are demons, there's no doubt about it.

WILLIAM JAMES

And it does no harm to repeat, as often as you can, 'Without me the literary industry would not exist: the publishers, the agents, the sub-agents, the sub-sub-agents, the accountants, the libel lawyers, the departments of literature, the professors, the theses, the books of criticism, the reviewers, the book pages—all this vast and proliferating edifice is because of this small, patronized, put-down and underpaid person.'

DORIS LESSING

. . . of making many books there is no end.

ECCLESIASTES 12:12

The revised edition of
THE WRITER'S QUOTATION BOOK
was designed by Hudson Studio,
Ossining, New York
and produced by James Charlton Associates,
New York, New York.

PUSHCART